# FUNDAMENTAL BOOK
# OF SIGIL MAGICK
# Vol. 3

## THE COMPENDIUM
## A Directory of Magick Sigils

K.P. Theodore

**Erebus Society**

# Erebus Society

First published in Great Britain in 2023
Erebus Society

First Edition

ISBN: 978-1-912461-49-3

www.ErebusSociety.com

# TABLE OF CONTENTS

# INDEX OF SIGILS

## MENTAL - SELF

# MENTAL - MIND

# MENTAL - DIVINATION

# MENTAL - PROTECTION

# MENTAL - POWER

# MENTAL - MISCELLANEOUS

# PHYSICAL - PEOPLE

# PHYSICAL - EMOTIONS & FEELINGS

# PHYSICAL - PLANTS

## PHYSICAL - CRYSTALS & MINERALS

# PHYSICAL - METALS

# PHYSICAL - ELEMENTS

# PHYSICAL - ESSENCES & QUALITIES

# PHYSICAL - MAGICK TOOLS

# PHYSICAL - DIVINATION

# PHYSICAL - PROTECTION

# PHYSICAL - CREATURES

# PHYSICAL - SABBATHS

# PHYSICAL - SEVEN DEADLY SINS

# PHYSICAL - SPELLS & RITUALS

# PREFACE

## Plato's World of Ideas

What is the world's fundamental reality? Ideas are the fundamental realities, according to the great philosopher and thinker Plato. There are many particular things in this world, but if we simply look at them in that way, nothing general can be drawn from them. Consequently, Plato categorises certain objects into many classes based on their shared characteristics. Concepts are nothing more than fundamental characteristics shared by every member of these classes.

As an illustration, there is a class of men, and each one of them possesses a quality known as manliess. As a result, the concept of manhood exists. Similar to this, there are several notions, such as the idea of an animal, beauty, or a piece of furniture, etc.

Plato says that this concept is of utmost importance if we want to be able to understand the meaning of sentences and have the ability to communicate with each other in a clear manner.

For example, if we say "Greece is the birthplace of Democracy", we need to have a clear understanding of the idea of "What is Greece?", "What does birth mean and what is the idea of a physical place?", "What does the idea of Democracy really mean?"... etc.

As ideas are the ultimate realities of the world, they are substances. Ideas are everlasting because they exist beyond space and time . Concepts predate specific things and exist separately from them. Ideas are many in number.

Plato claims that there is a different world of thoughts, also called "The World" of ideas. Our reason can understand it, but the existence of this world of ideas is not reliant on us. By asserting that there are some universal laws present in human reason that serve as the basis for knowing, Plato thus lays the groundwork for rationalism. Plato, supports Objective Idealism by highlighting the fact that concepts do not depend on humans for their existence.

Ideas have been ranked according to how complete and comprehensive they are. The idea of the "ON" (God/higher consciousness) is an ultimate and perfect idea, thus sits on the top of the hierarchy of ideas.

But how did the world of ideas become the real world? What connection exists between the world of ideas and this one?

Plato has proposed two ideas: 1) The connection between appearance and reality 2) The Participation Concept in which Plato claimed that the world of ideas existed in actuality and that the physical world was merely a copy of it.

As a better example, in his book "The Republic", Plato is using the allegory of the cave, which is the following:

The allegory of Plato's Cave is a philosophical concept that describes the human condition and our perception of reality. The story goes like this:

Imagine a group of people who have lived their entire lives chained inside a dark cave, facing a wall. Behind them is a fire, and between the fire and the prisoners, there is a raised platform. On this platform, there are people who carry objects and statues that cast shadows on the wall in front of the prisoners.

The prisoners, unable to turn their heads, can only see the shadows and hear echoes of the objects being carried. They believe that these shadows and echoes are the only reality that exists. They have no idea that there is a whole world outside the cave.

One day, one of the prisoners is freed and is forced to leave the cave. As he ascends towards the light, his eyes are blinded by the brightness of the outside world. But gradually, he begins to see the world as it truly is, and he realizes that the shadows he saw in the cave were mere illusions.

He returns to the cave to tell the other prisoners about the real world, but they don't believe him. They think he's crazy because the shadows on the wall are the only reality they've ever known.

The allegory of the cave is a metaphor for the journey of the philosopher, who seeks to understand the true nature of reality. It suggests that the world we see around us is only a shadow of a greater reality, and that we must free ourselves from our own mental chains in order to see things as they truly are.

## The Sigil World of Ideas

The Universal Sigils are being used as the standard symbolic means of manifestation and connection between our world and the world of ideas. A Magickal teller between realities. They can be used to represent ideas in the physical world and carry the corresponding energies through from other planes of existence in order to manifest in our realm of existence.

These sigils can be used in spellwork, rituals, meditation, divination etc.

# SIGIL MAGICK & PRACTICES

A simple yet efficient way of implementing sigils in spell and ritual, is by using them as representations of ideas and concepts. They can be used to represent people, qualities, situations, aspects etc.

As an example, let's see a diagram of a ritual for a couple who wishes to start a happy and prosperous family. A simple way to represent everything would be to copy the corresponding sigils on parchment and place them among the other ingredients (according to one's path) that vary from herbs to crystals, and from candles to incense etc.

Here is the placement of the sigils:

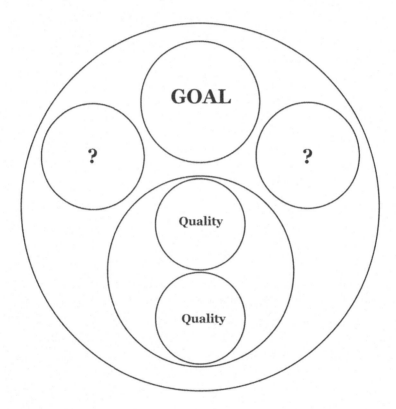

The large circle is the greater meaning of the ritual.

The two circles with the question mark are the "components" or the "parties".

The Goal circle is the main objective of the ritual.

The lower part includes the "Qualities" or "Essences" circle, which represent the specific attributes needed.

By replacing this table with words, one can create any possible variable they wish, but for the specific example here are the words needed:

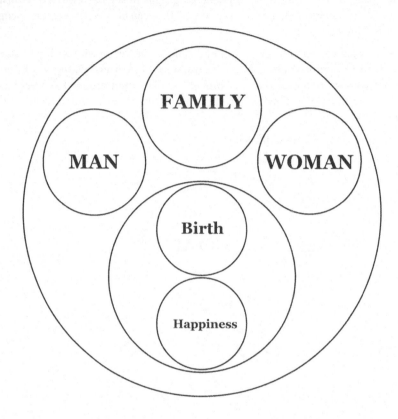

This represents the wish for the couple to create a happy family by using the birth of their first child as the starting point of this endeavour.

Once the words are placed in the corresponding circles (you can alter the formation of the circles and use as many as you need in your custom rituals), then the words are replaced by the corresponding sigils.

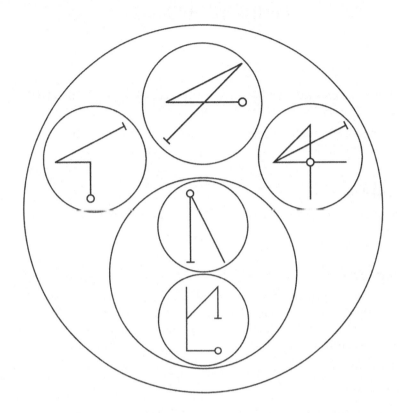

This could be used as a Master Sigil on its own or these can be used as individual elements on an altar during a ritual that requires more components and ingredients.

# SIGILS IN DIVINATION

One of the practices that have not been explained in the previous books, is the use of the Universal Sigils during Divination.

There are many ways in which on can implement the use of sigils in their Divinatory practices, the following are the most popular ones:

### Pendulum

A sigil of the intended quality can be placed under the pendulum mat or be used as a mat.

### Tasseography

A sigil of the intended quality can be placed under the cup or saucer that will be used for divination at the start of the session. This way, while the subject (person interested in the reading) enjoys their cup of coffee/tea, the entire practice is charged towards the particular interest.

### Oracle Deck

One can create their own custom oracle deck by drawing sigils of various meanings on plain cards. This is a way of developing one's very own system of divination that can be altered and adjusted according to their needs.

# SIGIL COMBINATION

A very common practice when it comes to universal sigils is to combine two or more sigils in order to create a new sigil with the combined essence/meaning of the sigils used as its components.

For example, if one wants to study without being stressed, they can combine the sigils for studying and relaxation in order to create a new sigil for their intended purpose. Each person will find their own way to do so, thus, the end result is custom to each practitioner.

# THE SIGILS COMPENDIUM

Here starts the catalog of Universal Sigils (in Alphabetical Order). For further information on the formation, use, mantra pronunciation, or details on the implementation of sigils, please consult the Volumes 1 and 2 of The Fundemantal Books of Sigil Magick.

# MENTAL SIGILS

### For one's Self

## TO ACCEPT A CHALLENGE

Mantra: PHELANGTOC

## TO ACCEPT THE TRUTH

Mantra: ACTOPERHU

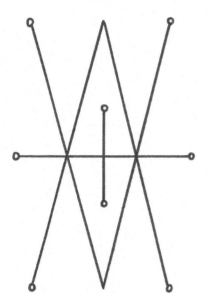

## TO BE MORE ACTIVE

Mantra: VECTIBA

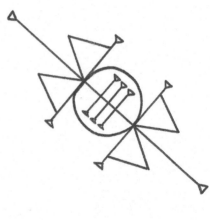

## TO ACKNOWLEDGE ONE'S BAD HABITS

Mantra: GOLM HAKT DWEB YSI

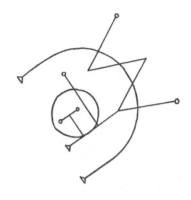

## TO MANAGE ONE'S BAD HABITS
Mantra: SHAMBYC GENTID

## BEHAVIOURAL CHANGE
Mantra:
GTARVHO MNEBUWSYCI

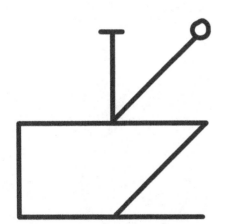

## CALM DOWN AFTER ARGUMENT
Mantra:
WRILCOM FHAGNETU

## FOR COMFORT
Mantra: GNARLOC FIEMT

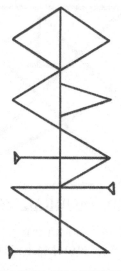

## TO PROMOTE CONFIDENCE

Mantra: CEBD FONTI

## TO BE MORE DARING

Mantra: DRACOM NIGBE

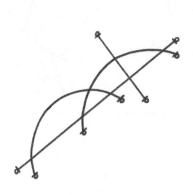

## TO PROMOTE DETERMINATION

Mantra: BER MINDT

## TO OBTAIN BETTER EATING HABITS

Mantra:
MAKHET SGOR BINC

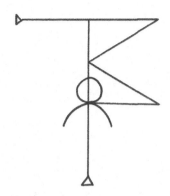

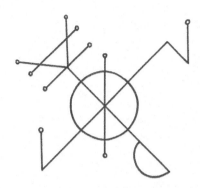

### TO PROMOTE ELOQUENCE

Mantra: LENTO BUQ

### FOR EMOTIONAL INDEPENDENCE

Mantra: TANEI MOLDYP

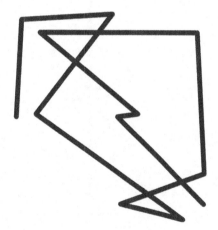

### TO FIND LOST ENTHUSIASM

Mantra: STEMIN FLODHUA

### TO FIND LOST EXCITEMENT

Mantra: XENDTOS FLIMC

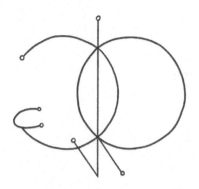

## TO BE MORE GENEROUS

Mantra: GARNEO UMIS

## TO FOLLOW A GOAL

Mantra: LAWNT HEI GOF

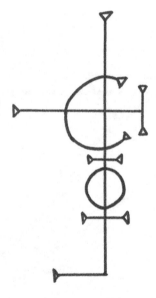

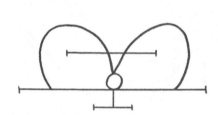

## TO SET A GOAL

Mantra: PEL GHASTO

## TO BE HEALTHIER

Mantra: COMBE HALTIR

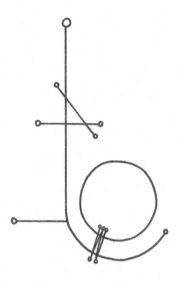

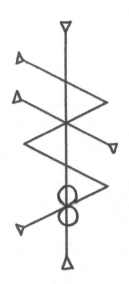

### TO BE MORE JOYFUL

Mantra: YJAMO ULIF

### TO LEARN A NEW SKILL

Mantra: NAWRGIS KEL

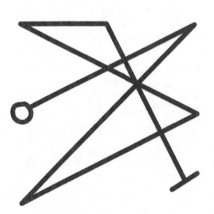

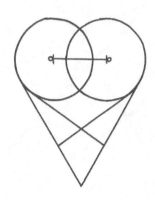

### TO LEARN FASTER

Mantra: ELFNIM STRAG

### TO INSTILL THE LOVE OF LEARNING

Mantra: NARGOL VEI

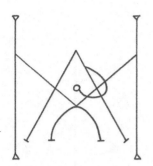

## TO ENHANCE THE CURRENT STATE OF LUCK

Mantra:
HAR MUNTYC LEK

## TO MASTER A SKILL

Mantra: KLEMSTARI

## MORAL CHASTITY

Mantra: ALCHIR STOMY

## MORAL FREEDOM

Mantra: ELFAR DOM

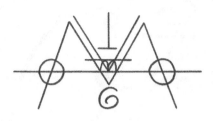

## FOR MOTIVATION

Mantra: MORBING TVAO

## TO OPEN UP

Mantra: PUNTOE

## TO OVERCOME BITTERNESS

Mantra: STREVIN COMB

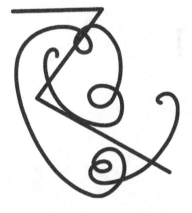

## TO OVERCOME DESPAIR

Mantra: PASDREM VICO

### TO OVERCOME DISAPPOINTMENT

Mantra:
DRANSTI MEVCOP

### TO OVERCOME FAILURE

Mantra:
LAFREMO CUVI

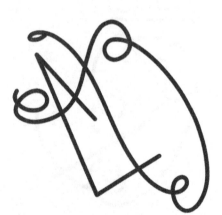

### TO OVERCOME FEAR

Mantra: VORCFA ME

### TO OVERCOME FRUSTRATION

Mantra: FREMSTAN VOUCI

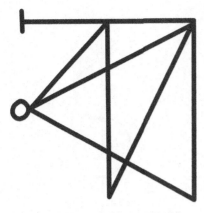

## TO OVERCOME LOSS

Mantra: RAVC METHILOS

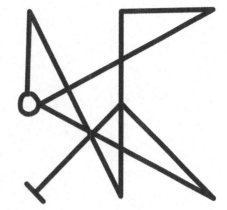

## TO OVERCOME MOURNING

Mantra: RAVCOT SHMIGEN

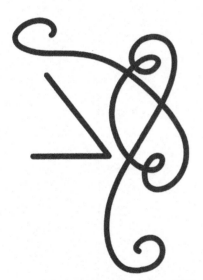

## TO OVERCOME SORROW

Mantra: SREWM COV

## TO OVERCOME WORRY

Mantra: WROVY CEM

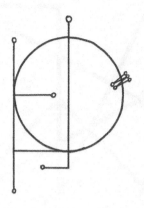

## TO BE MORE PEACEFUL

Mantra: FELAC PUMI

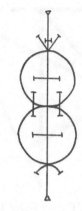

## TO RECOGNISE PROBABILITIES

Mantra: PHERLING BOSTA

## TO INCREASE PRODUCTIVITY
Mantra:
ESPOR NICA DYVTU

## TO FIND PRODUCTIVITY
Mantra:
BERCOMP DVUTI

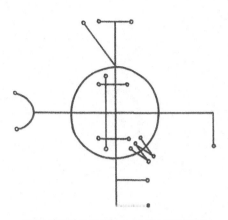

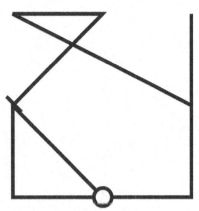

## TO FOLLOW A ROUTINE

Mantra:
LWITH NUG FERO

## SELF-ESTEEM AID

Mantra: EMGRALS FTHIV

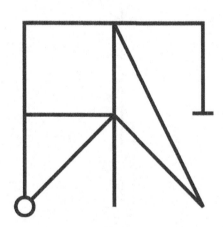

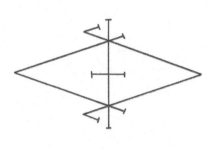

## SELF-WORTH AID

Mantra:
VILGRAMNU THYWES

## TO BE MORE SENSITIVE

Mantra: VENTA MIS

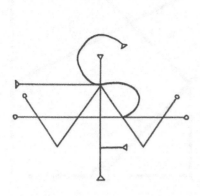

## TO SLEEP MORE EASILY

Mantra: LHEMP FASIR

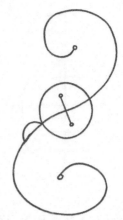

## TO BE MORE STABLE

Mantra: IB CELMO SAT

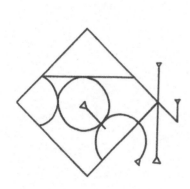

## FOR STIMULATION

Mantra: NARET GIMOLULS

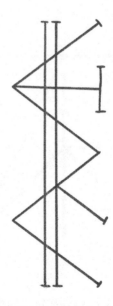

## TO STUDY HARDER

Mantra: KESTHUR MADY

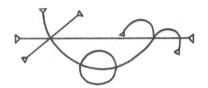

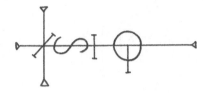

## TO BE MORE SYSTEMATIC

Mantra: CRAST OMY EI

## ENGAGEMENT TO TASKS

Mantra: NEH GAITOSK

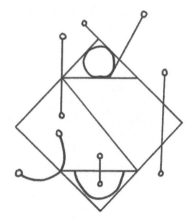

## TO DISCOVER
## ONE'S TRUE SELF

Mantra: NULIFUS DRETO

## TO ACKNOWLEDGE
## ONE'S TRUE SELF

Mantra:
KLEM DOGRAW TUSYF

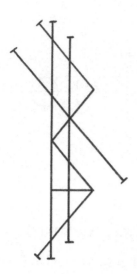

## TO WORK HARDER

Mantra: DHAWR KEMO

# MENTAL SIGILS

### For the Mind

### AGAINST ANXIETY

Mantra: XENSTIGAY

### AGAINST STRESS

Mantra: GINESTRA

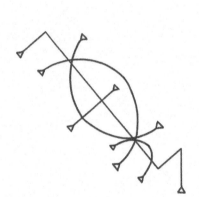

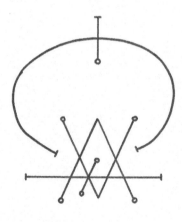

### TO PROMOTE CALMNESS

Mantra: CELMBA

### FOR CLARITY

Mantra: THEVA CIRLY

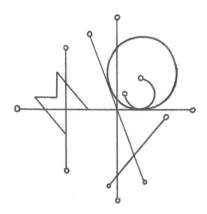

## FOR CLEAR THOUGHTS

Mantra:
PYCT FOWHI NARGLEM

## FOR CONCENTRATION

Mantra: OMPRI VENTAC

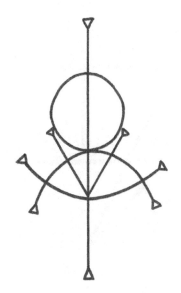

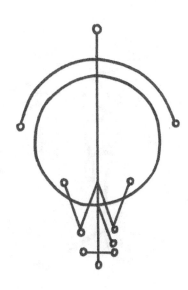

## TO BE MORE CONSCIOUS

Mantra: CORM BE NISU

## TO PROMOTE CREATIVITY

Mantra: MARCIT EVOY

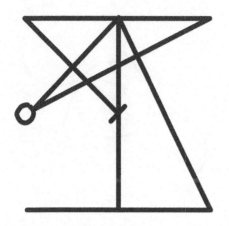

### DECISION AID

Mantra: MITHAD GNECKO

### FOR EMOTIONAL RELIEF

Mantra:
NEID VOM LYRAT

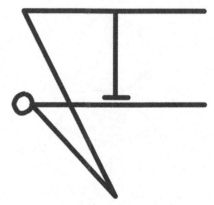

### EMOTIONAL STABILITY

Mantra: MALTOS NIEBY

### FINDING A SOLUTION

Mantra: FTAUVNI DOH

## TO AID FOCUSING

Mantra:
GAWN SCODI FTUH

## HEALING MINDSET

Mantra: STLAMDE NIGH

## INNER PEACE

Mantra: PACRENI

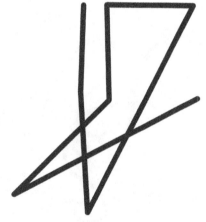

## INNER STRENGTH

Mantra: GHERTSNI

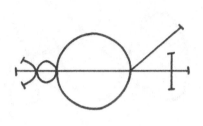

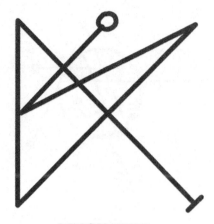

## TO PROMOTE INSPIRATION

Mantra: MONIS PARTE

## LINGUISTIC PERCEPTION AID

Mantra: ADRESTAL NUI

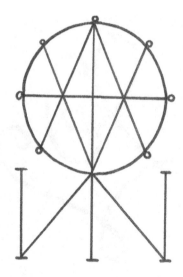

## TO MANAGE ANGER

Mantra: GREMNA

## FOR MEDITATION

Mantra: VERPIM TANDO

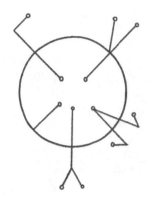

## MEMORY

Mantra: OM ERY GNAL

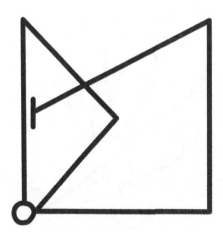

## MENTAL DECLUTTERING

Mantra: SYCLORA NEDIM

## MENTAL BANISHING

Mantra: GINTA BELMSH

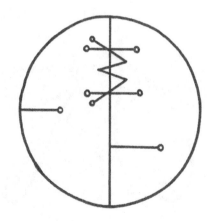

## MENTAL HEALING

Mantra: LENHIGTAM

### MENTAL BALANCE

Mantra: MBLENTAC

### MENTAL ESCAPE

Mantra: PLEMSCANT

### MENTAL GROWTH

Mantra: THRAW GLEMNO

### MENTAL RELIEF

Mantra: FLARNI TEM

## MENTAL STABILITY

Mantra: BLYSMAN TIEL

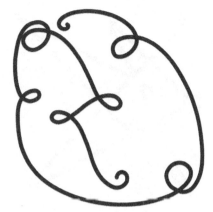

## MINDFULNESS

Mantra: SLENDU FIM

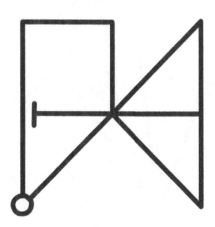

## MOOD BOOST

Mantra:
PLAEDORIS FTYMNUC

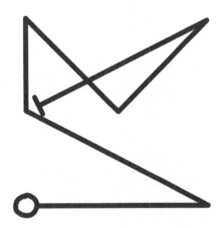

## MUSICAL PERCEPTION AID

Mantra: DULCONAM PERIC

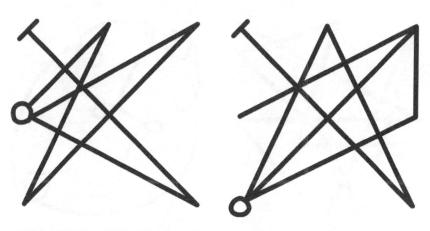

## ORGANISE AND PLAN AID

Mantra: MERTOPLIN GASD

## PATTERN PERCEPTION AID

Mantra:
STREN XAPLOM CIG

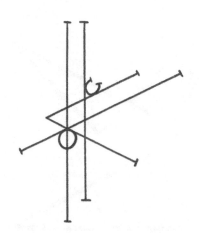

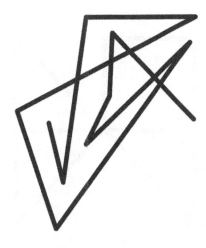

## TO AID ONE'S PERCEPTION

Mantra: VAHTIP BERCON

## QUICKER THINKING

Mantra: GRENTHCK IQU

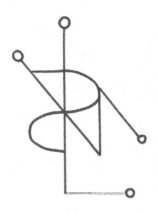

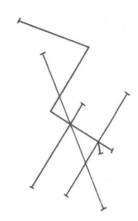

## FOR RELAXATION

Mantra: DIX ARMEL

## RITUAL MINDSET

Mantra: MEDTAR LINUS

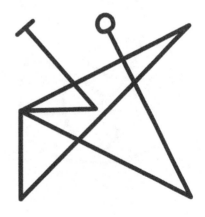

## SERENITY

Mantra: VERACHNIO TYS

## SPATIAL PERCEPTION AID

Mantra: TRAGMEPC DIVONS

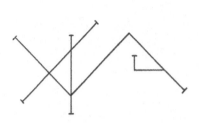

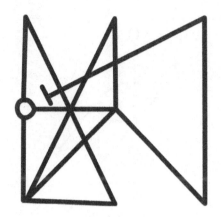

**SPELL MINDSET**

Mantra: CANDTIP SGELM

**SPIRITUAL PERCEPTION AID**

Mantra:
GHESPAWM CICLUV TOND

**SPIRITUAL GROWTH**

Mantra: THORGAWL SIPU

**STUDY MINDSET**

Mantra: DINSTU MEY

### SUBCONSCIOUS EXPLORATION
Mantra:
SULATRIPEX BONC

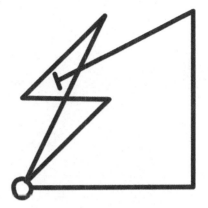

### TEMPORAL PERCEPTION AID
Mantra: MANTRIV PEGC

### TO UNLOCK INNER POWER
Mantra: WIRPUNCK LON

# MENTAL SIGILS

For Divination

## CHARTOMANCY

Mantra: MARCHON VIDTY

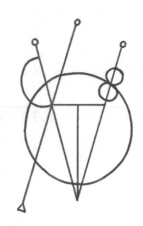

## AID FOR DIVINATION IN GENERAL

Mantra: VANDOT BIS

## HIEROMANCY

Mantra: NAHRECOM VIDTY

## RUNES

Mantra: STRAN VOUEDI

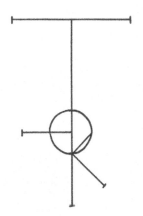

## TAROT READINGS AID

Mantra: FORTENT GAI

## TEA LEAVES

Mantra: ADTLES VONI

# MENTAL SIGILS

For Protection

## PROTECTION FROM BAD DECISIONS
Mantra:
CROMPTIS FDEBAN

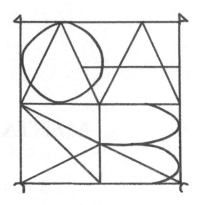

## PROTECTION FROM EVENTS OF BAD LUCK
Mantra:
FEMBAN DRIKT PULCO

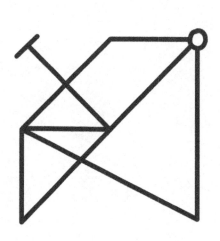

## PROTECTION FROM EMOTIONAL TURBULENCE
Mantra:
SCLITUPAWN DOFREM

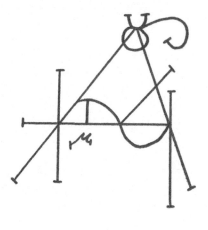

## GENERAL PROTECTION

Mantra:
DRAMLOC PITHEG

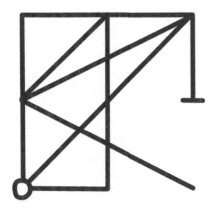

## PROTECTION FROM LOW SELF-ESTEEM

Mantra:
SHATBONFLIV GRUMCYDEP

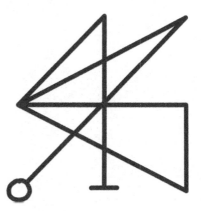

## PROTECTION FROM NEGATIVE THOUGHTS

Mantra:
DTRACHIGN POVEFK

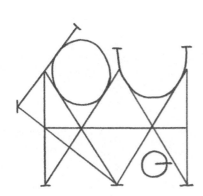

## PROTECTION FROM NIGHTMARES

Mantra:
GHRASFEM PICTO

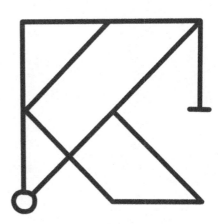

## PROTECTION FROM SELF-HARM

Mantra:
GNISHTRO PLECADO FLYM

# MENTAL SIGILS

### For Power

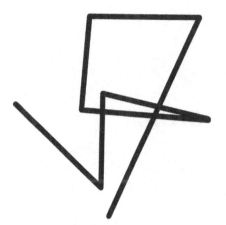

## ASTRAL PLANE ACCESS
Mantra: STREPNAC

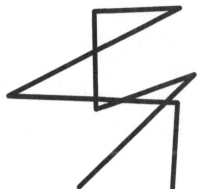

## ASTRAL PLANE SAFETY
Mantra: FYLTRENPAS

## AURIC CLEANSING
Mantra: GLENRAUCIS

## AURIC MANIPULATION
Mantra: PLATRICUMNO

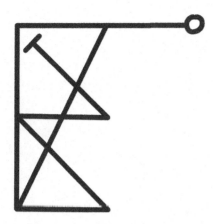

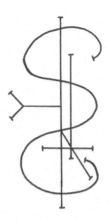

## DIMENSIONAL JUMPING

Mantra:
PELJONSCAG BHUMD

## TO ENHANCE ABILITIES

Mantra: STRENYM BLICHAD

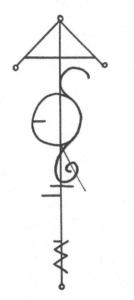

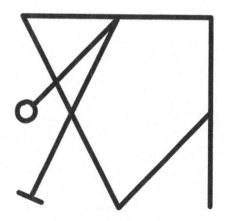

## TO RAISE POWER

Mantra: FERTIS POGNAW

## REALITY SHIFT

Mantra: LHARTOB MESIFY

# MENTAL SIGILS

<u>Miscellaneous</u>

### BRAVERY

Mantra: MARBETOV

### COMMUNICATION

Mantra: MANTREB CUFOI

### COMPASSION

Mantra: AMDRE FICTOPS

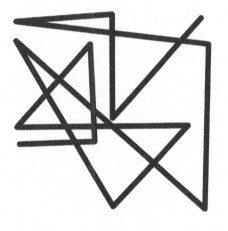

### DISCIPLINE

Mantra: BERDTOMS PLINC

### DO AS THOU WILT

Mantra: STLAU DHOWI

### EFFICIENCY

Mantra: TREMPO VICNYF

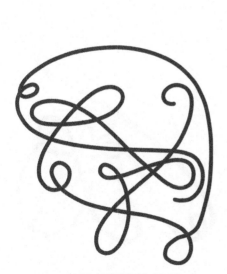

### FAMILY BONDING

Mantra: BANGDIL FOMY

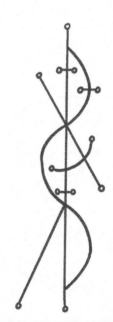

### FOR FRIENDSHIP

Mantra: PARSH FEIND

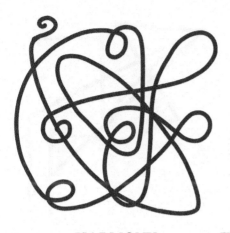

### HARMONY
Mantra: CTANY HIEVOM

### TO HEAL AFTER A BREAKUP
Mantra: FLUTH PABEK

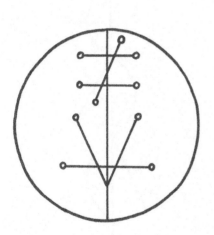

### GENERAL HEALING AID
Mantra: GALINHED

### HONESTY
Mantra: THEONYS

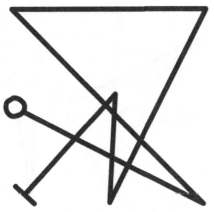

## TO IDENTIFY CHANCES

Mantra: HADROIST NEC

## TO IDENTIFY OPPORTUNITY

Mantra:
SHPRUDCA IGNYTOE

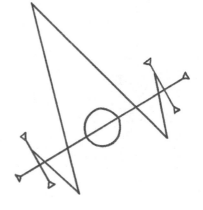

## SIGIL OF LEARNING SIGILS

Mantra: RONSIE GLAF

## TO BANISH NEGATIVITY

Mantra: VESHTA

### FOR NEGATIVITY

Mantra: SVUNGER THO JABYC

### PERSISTENCE

Mantra: STREMPO BINC

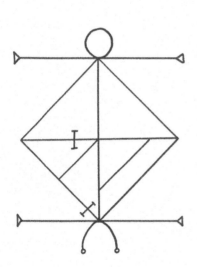

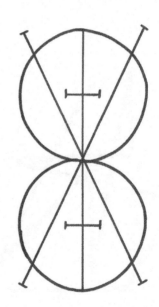

### FOR POSITIVITY

Mantra:
SVERN BYOPT GHUJIC

### TO FAVOUR PROBABILITIES

Mantra:
GERVUD TIB PALFOS

### RECONCILIATION

Mantra: FTERP LONCIA

### SPIRITUAL PURITY

Mantra: LYASPUTRI

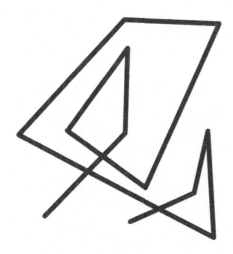

### SIGIL OF THE TEACHER

Mantra: HERCATILF GOS

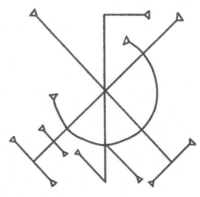

### FOR THE TRUTH

Mantra: DRENT SULHAF

## WISH AFFIRMATION

Mantra: TRONFINS HAW

# PHYSICAL SIGILS

Representations of People

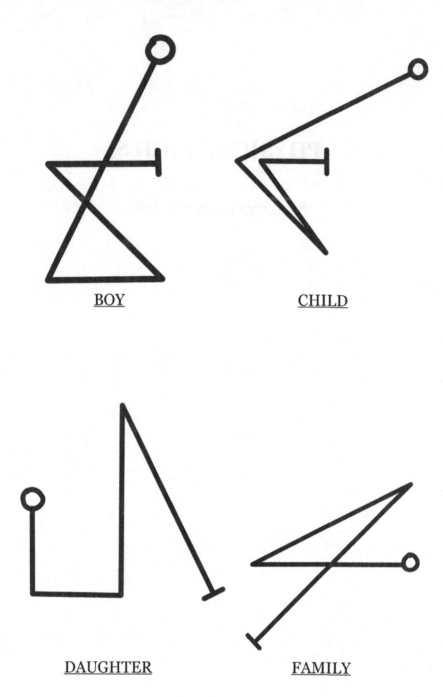

BOY

CHILD

DAUGHTER

FAMILY

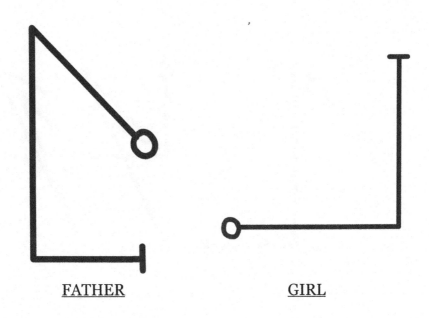

FATHER                    GIRL

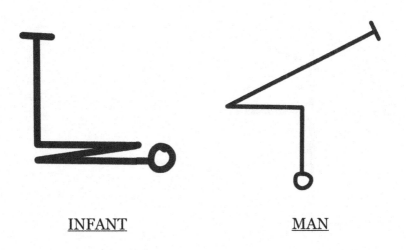

INFANT                    MAN

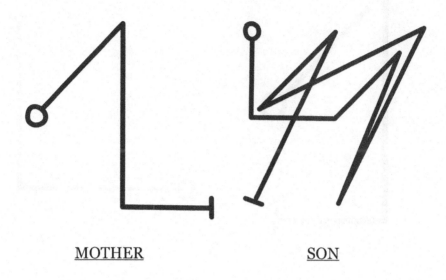

MOTHER                    SON

WOMAN

# PHYSICAL SIGILS

## Representations of Emotions & Feelings

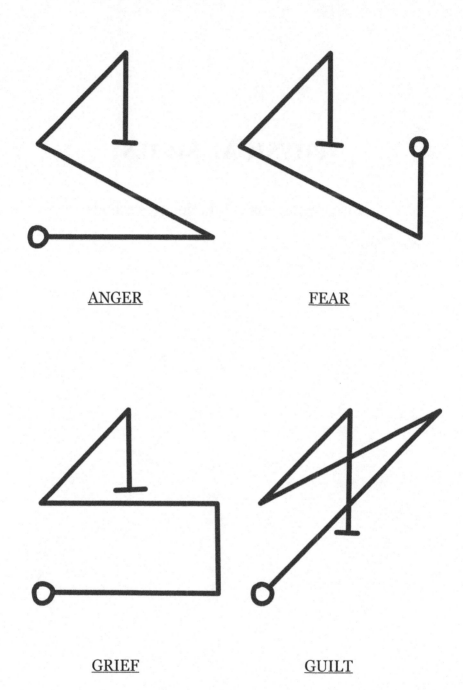

ANGER           FEAR

GRIEF           GUILT

HAPPINESS

HATE

JOY

LOVE

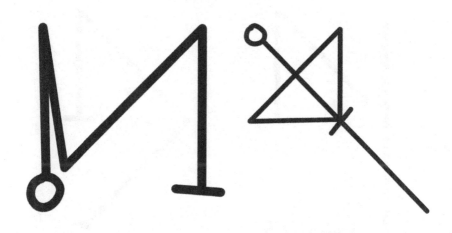

SADNESS                    SORROW

# PHYSICAL SIGILS

## Representations of Plants

ACONITE

AGRIMONY

ALFALFA

ANGELICA ROOT

ARROWROOT                    ASAFOETIDA

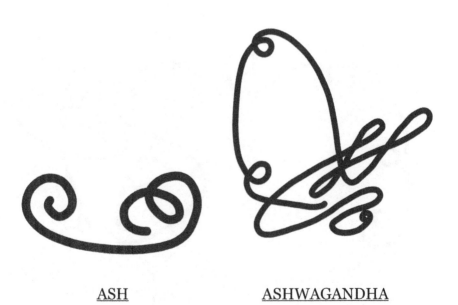

ASH                    ASHWAGANDHA

BASIL                    BAY

BIRCH            BLADDERWRACK

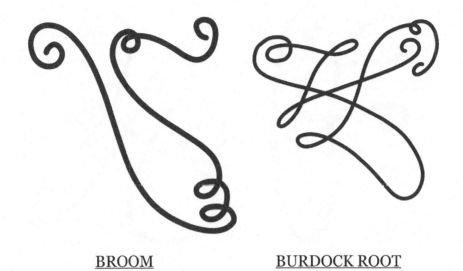

BROOM                    BURDOCK ROOT

CARAWAY                  CARNATION

CEDAR          CHAMOMILE

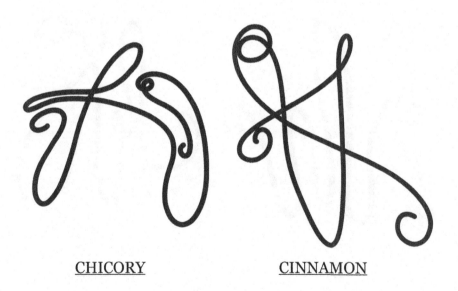

CHICORY          CINNAMON

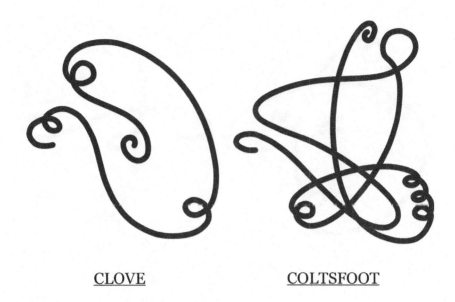

<u>CLOVE</u>  <u>COLTSFOOT</u>

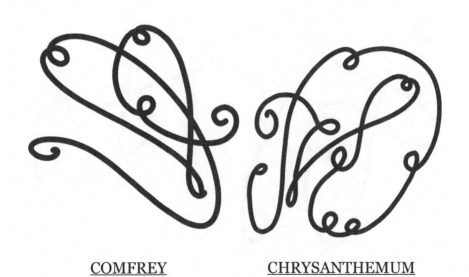

<u>COMFREY</u>  <u>CHRYSANTHEMUM</u>

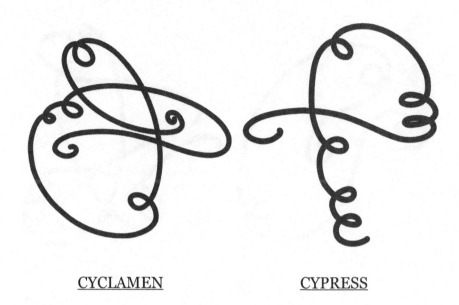

CYCLAMEN

CYPRESS

DANDELION

DOGWOOD

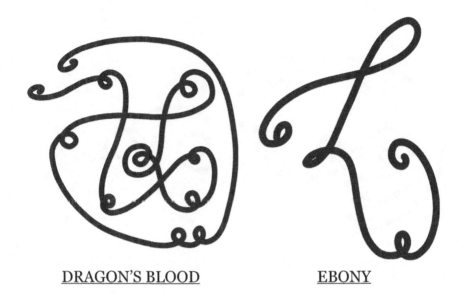

DRAGON'S BLOOD          EBONY

ELDER          ELDERFLOWER

73

EUCALYPTUS                    FENNEL

FENUGREEK                    FIGWORT

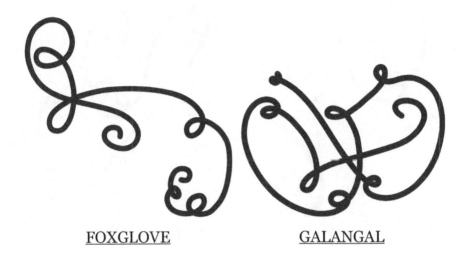

FOXGLOVE          GALANGAL

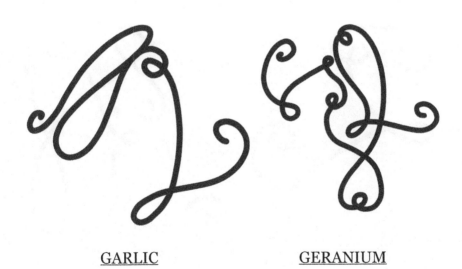

GARLIC          GERANIUM

GINKO

GOLDENROD

GOURD

HAWTHORN

HAZEL                    HEATHER

HENNA                    HIBISCUS

HOLLY                    HYACINTH

HYSSOP                   IVY

JUNIPER          KAVA-KAVA

LAUREL          LAVENDER

LEMON BALM                    LEMONGRASS

LILY                          LINSEED

LIVERWORT          LOTUS

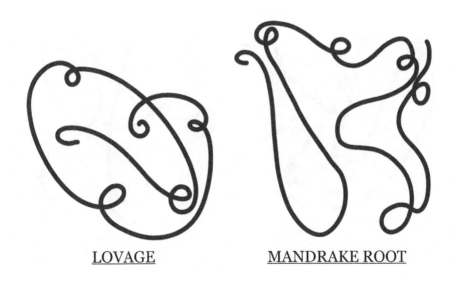

LOVAGE          MANDRAKE ROOT

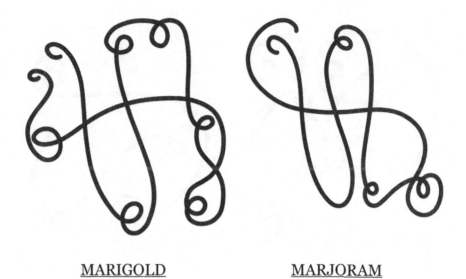

MARIGOLD          MARJORAM

MEADOWSWEET          MISTLETOE

MUGWORT                    MYRRH

NETTLE                     OAK

OLIVE

ORRIS

PEPPERMINT

ROSE

ROSEMARY                    SAGE

SANDALWOOD          ST. JOHN'S WORT

THISTLE                    THYME

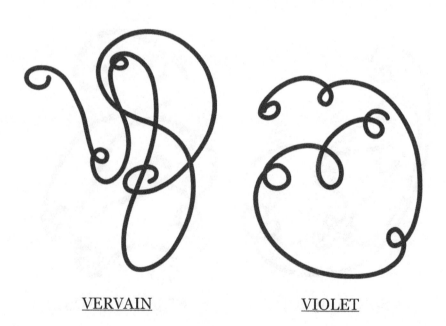

VERVAIN                    VIOLET

WALNUT    WILLOW

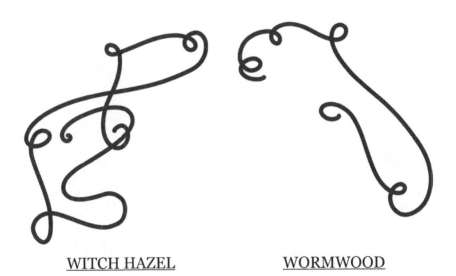

WITCH HAZEL    WORMWOOD

YARROW                    YEW

# PHYSICAL SIGILS

Representations of Crystals & Minerals

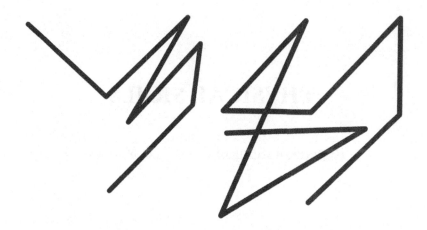

AGATE - BANDED        AGATE - CRAZY LACE

AGATE - MOSS        AGATE - TURRITELLA

AMAZONITE

AMBER

AMETHYST

AQUAMARINE

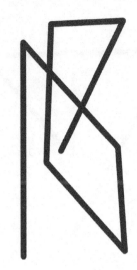

ARAGONITE

AZURITE

BLOODSTONE

CARNELIAN

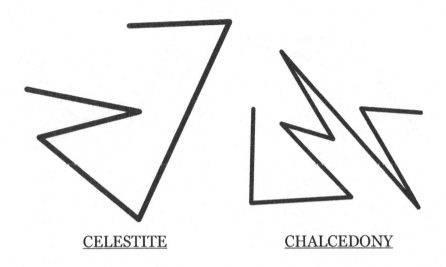

CELESTITE                    CHALCEDONY

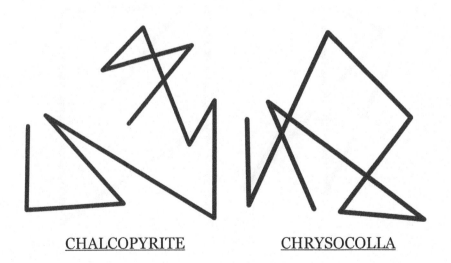

CHALCOPYRITE                 CHRYSOCOLLA

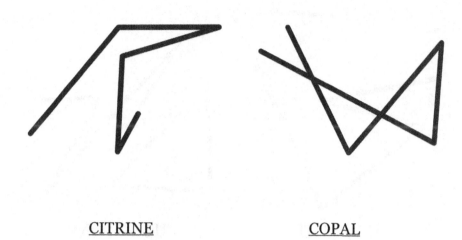

CITRINE          COPAL

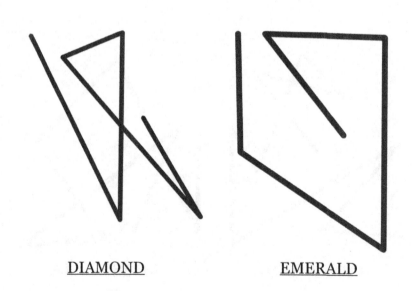

DIAMOND          EMERALD

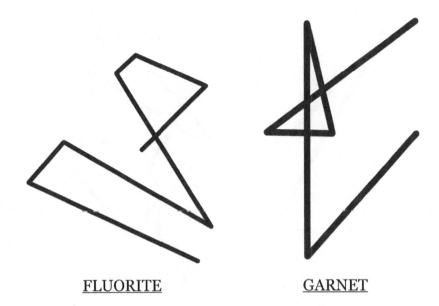

FLUORITE          GARNET

HEMATITE          HOWLITE

JADE

JASPER - AUTUMN

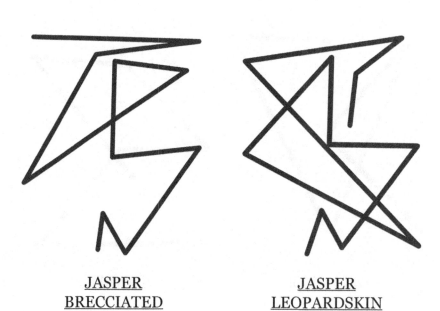

JASPER
BRECCIATED

JASPER
LEOPARDSKIN

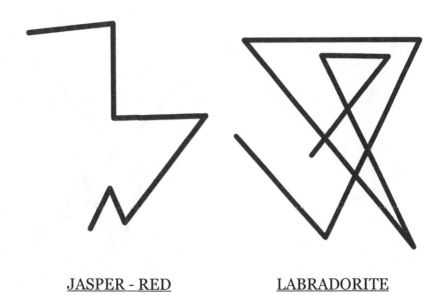

**JASPER - RED**  **LABRADORITE**

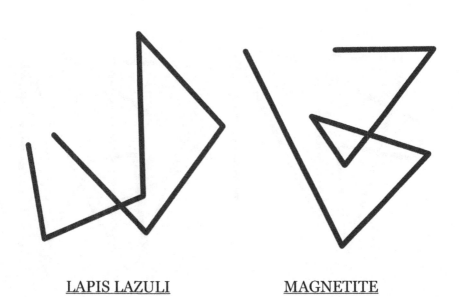

**LAPIS LAZULI**  **MAGNETITE**

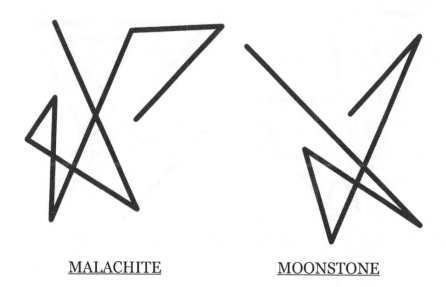

MALACHITE          MOONSTONE

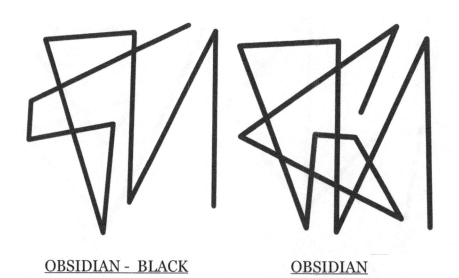

OBSIDIAN - BLACK        OBSIDIAN
                       SNOWFLAKE

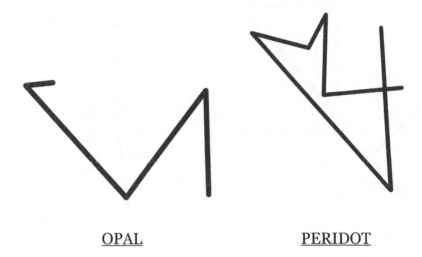

OPAL          PERIDOT

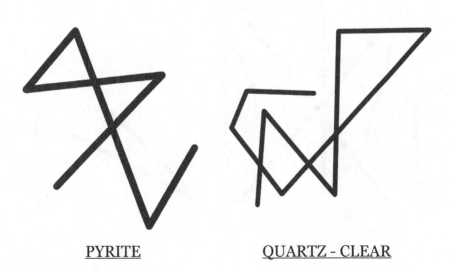

PYRITE          QUARTZ - CLEAR

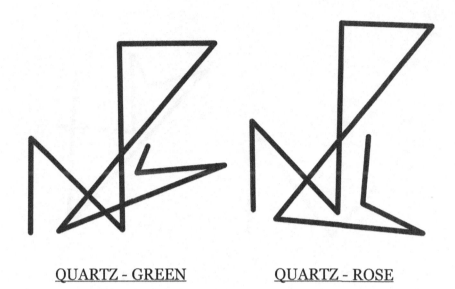

QUARTZ - GREEN          QUARTZ - ROSE

QUARTZ - SMOKY          RUBY

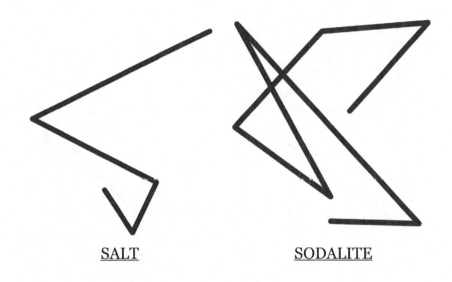

SALT                SODALITE

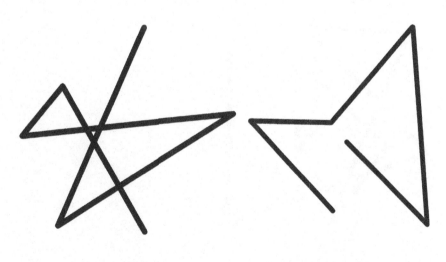

SULPHUR          SUNSTONE

101

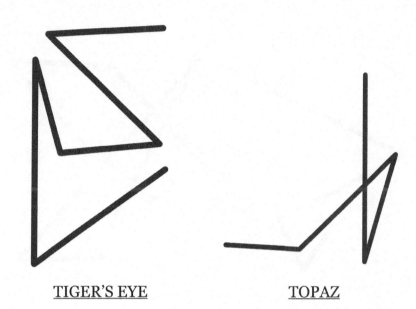

TIGER'S EYE              TOPAZ

TOURMALINE

# PHYSICAL SIGILS

## Representations of Metals

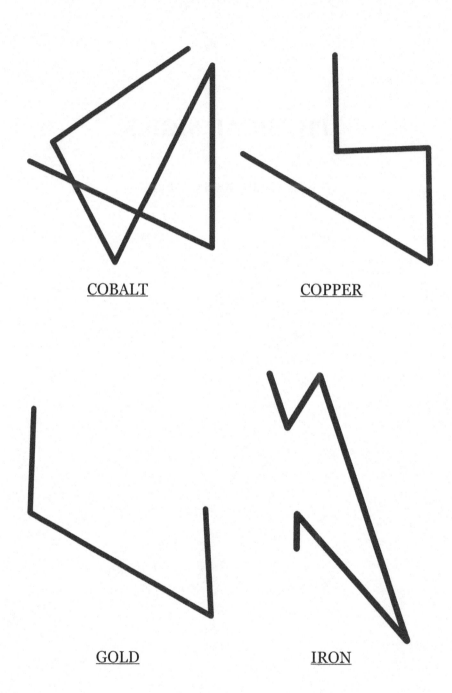

COBALT

COPPER

GOLD

IRON

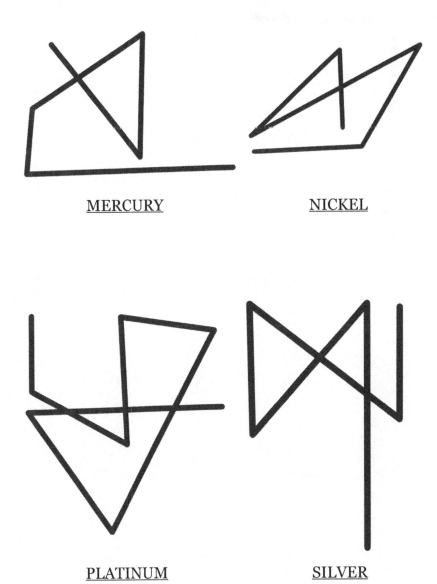

MERCURY

NICKEL

PLATINUM

SILVER

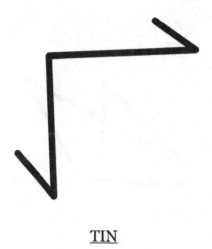

TIN

# PHYSICAL SIGILS

## Representations of Elements

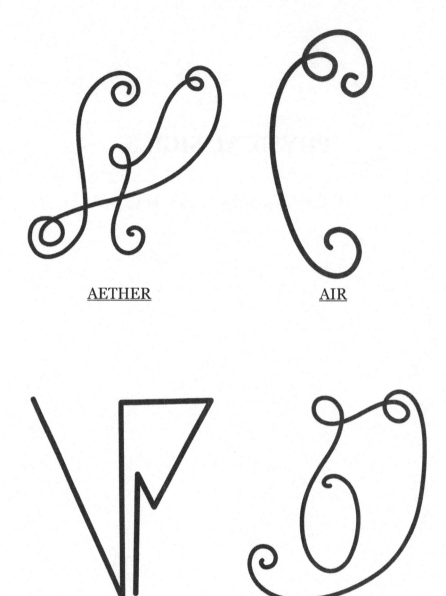

AETHER

AIR

DARKNESS

EARTH

FIRE

LIGHT

METAL

SPIRIT

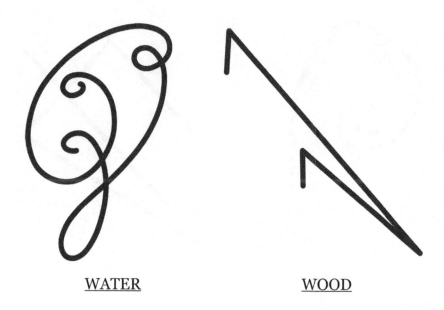

WATER

WOOD

# PHYSICAL SIGILS

## Representations of Essences & Qualities

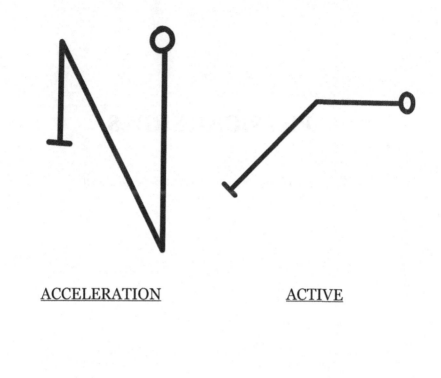

ACCELERATION                    ACTIVE

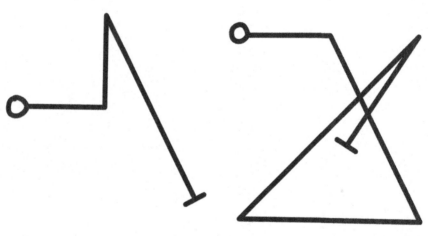

ADVENTURE                    ASTRAL PLANE

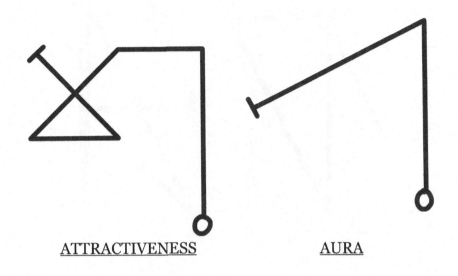

ATTRACTIVENESS          AURA

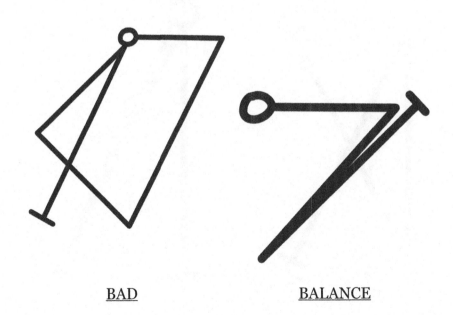

BAD                    BALANCE

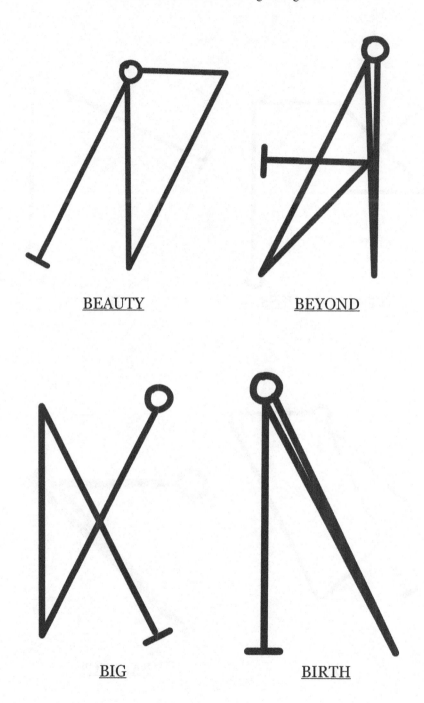

BEAUTY         BEYOND

BIG         BIRTH

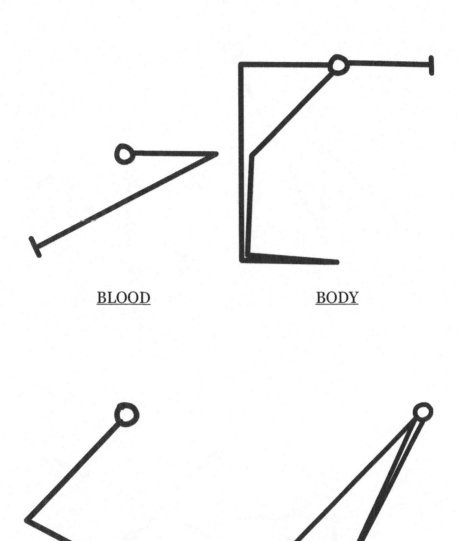

BLOOD                     BODY

BRAVERY               CHALLENGE

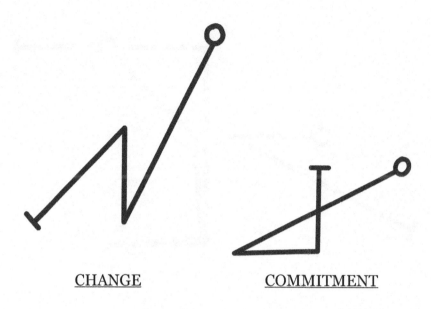

CHANGE          COMMITMENT

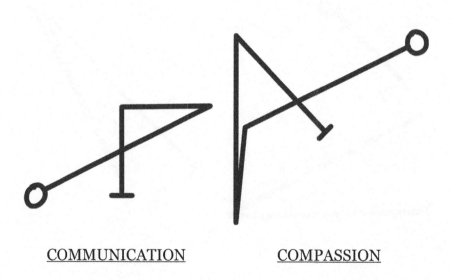

COMMUNICATION          COMPASSION

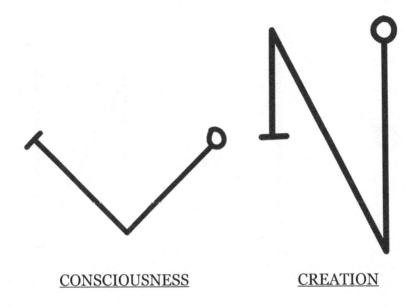

CONSCIOUSNESS     CREATION

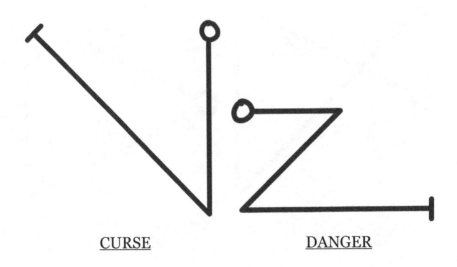

CURSE     DANGER

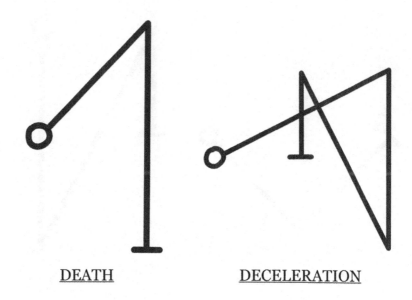

DEATH                    DECELERATION

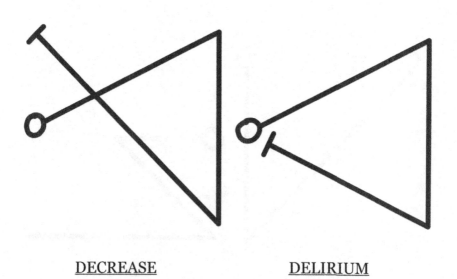

DECREASE                 DELIRIUM

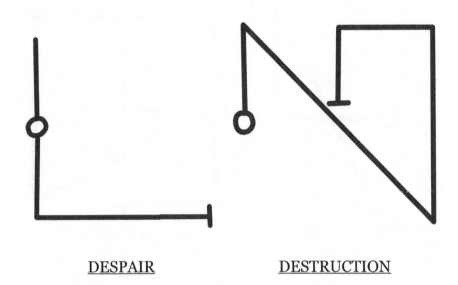

DESPAIR             DESTRUCTION

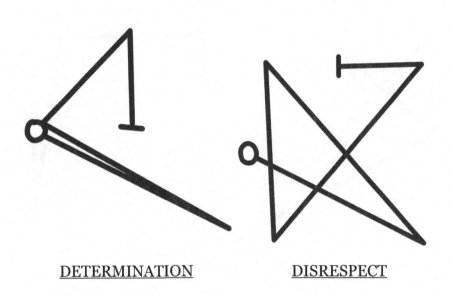

DETERMINATION       DISRESPECT

119

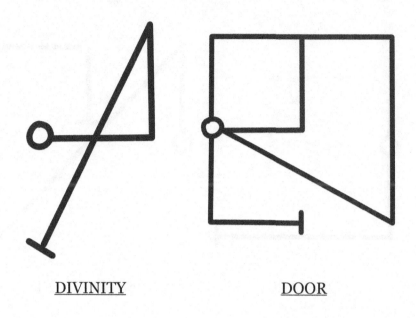

DIVINITY                    DOOR

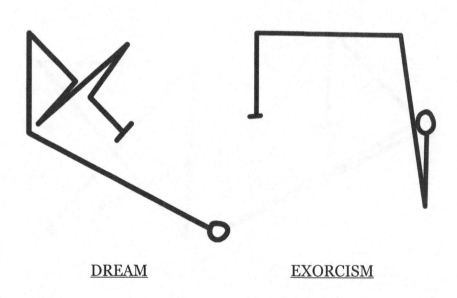

DREAM                    EXORCISM

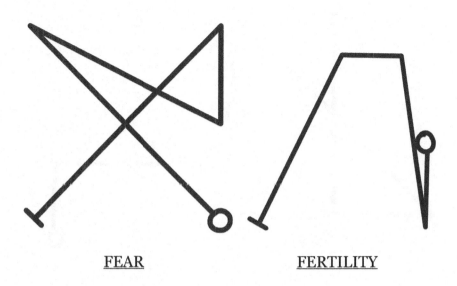

FEAR          FERTILITY

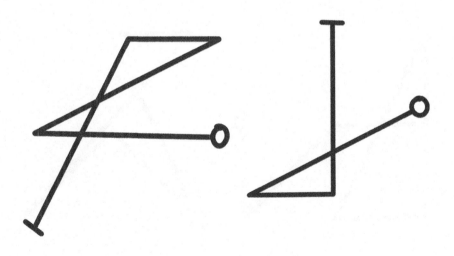

FIDELITY          FIGHT

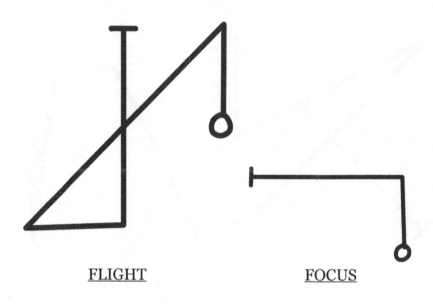

FLIGHT                    FOCUS

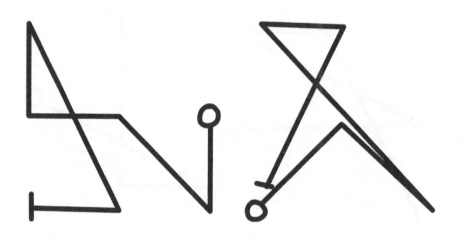

FRIENDSHIP            GENEROSITY

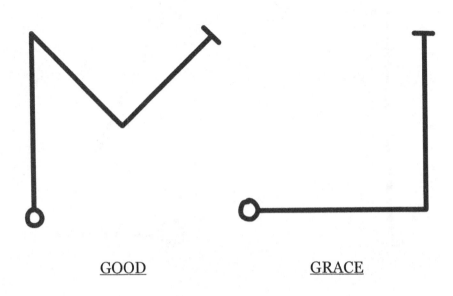

GOOD          GRACE

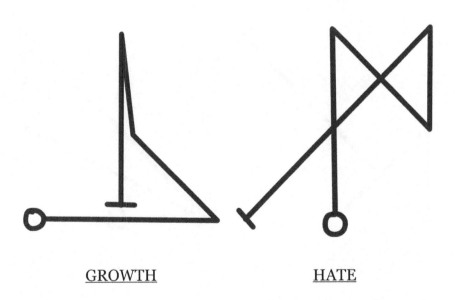

GROWTH          HATE

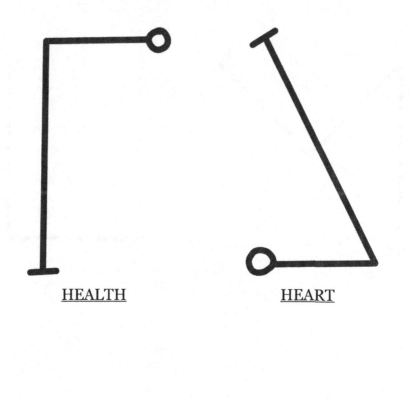

HEALTH

HEART

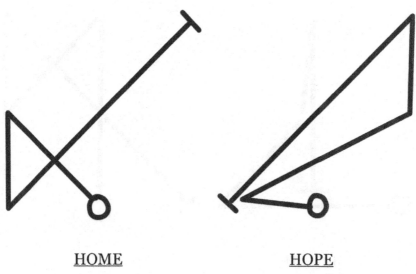

HOME

HOPE

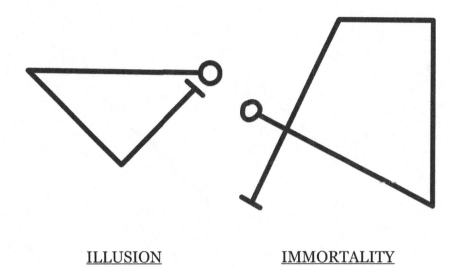

ILLUSION            IMMORTALITY

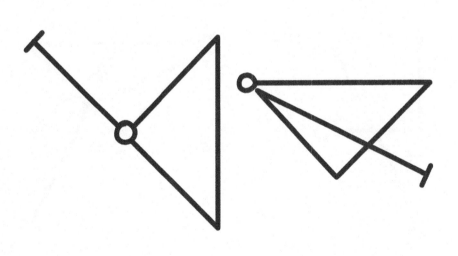

INCREASE            INJUSTICE

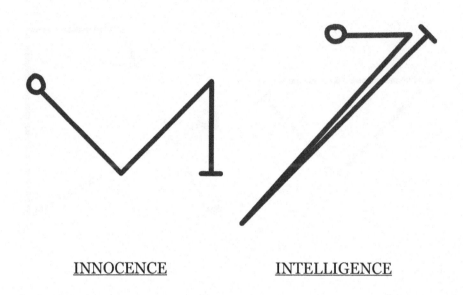

INNOCENCE                    INTELLIGENCE

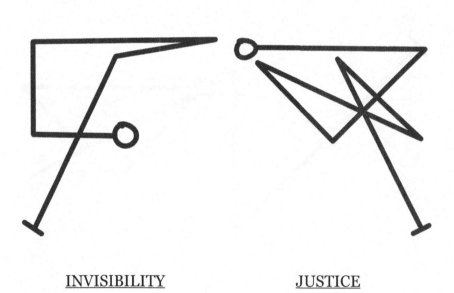

INVISIBILITY                    JUSTICE

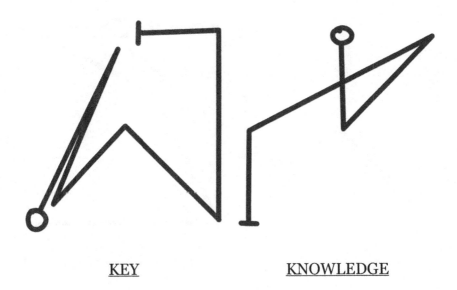

KEY               KNOWLEDGE

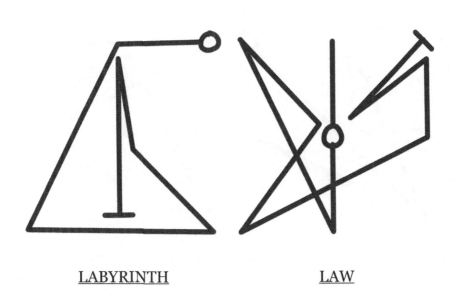

LABYRINTH          LAW

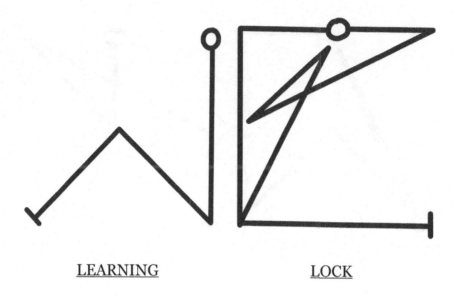

LEARNING             LOCK

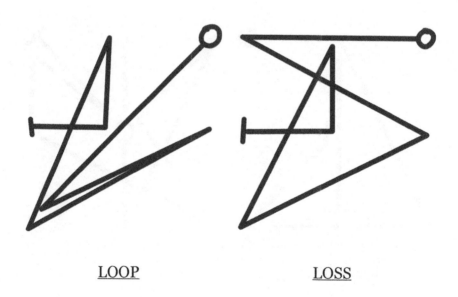

LOOP                 LOSS

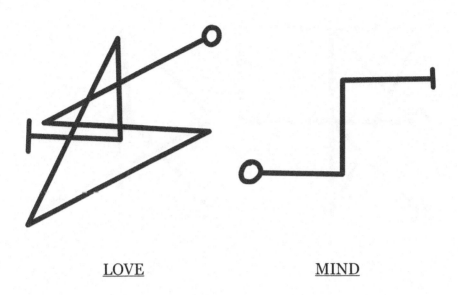

LOVE                    MIND

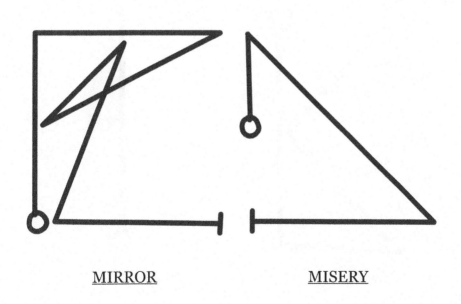

MIRROR                  MISERY

129

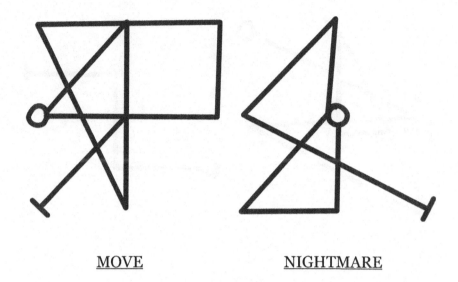

MOVE                    NIGHTMARE

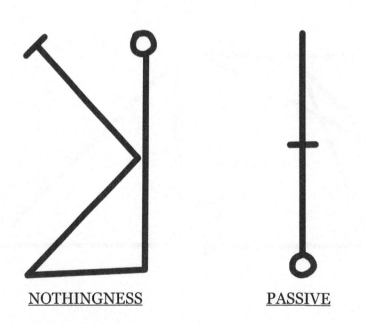

NOTHINGNESS              PASSIVE

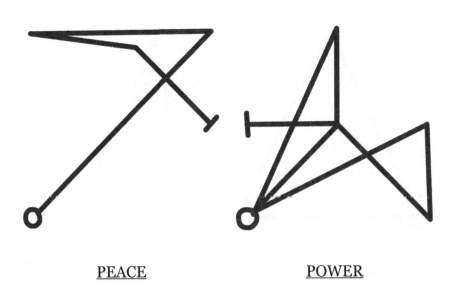

PEACE          POWER

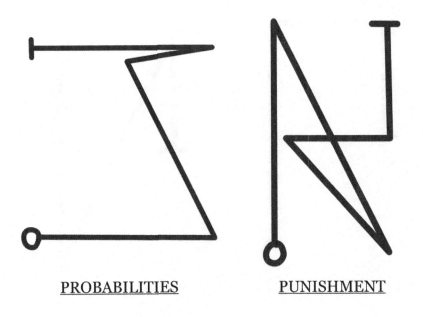

PROBABILITIES          PUNISHMENT

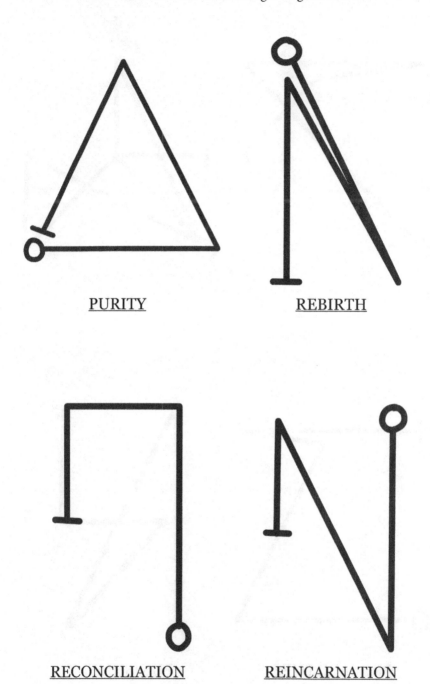

PURITY

REBIRTH

RECONCILIATION

REINCARNATION

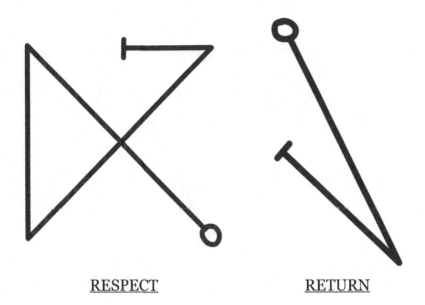

RESPECT                    RETURN

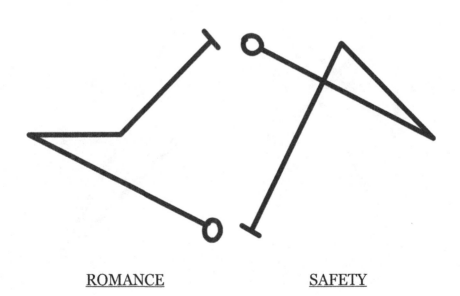

ROMANCE                    SAFETY

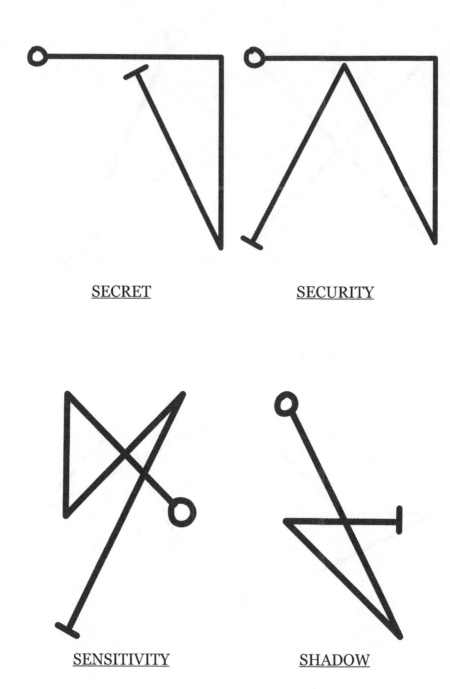

SECRET                    SECURITY

SENSITIVITY               SHADOW

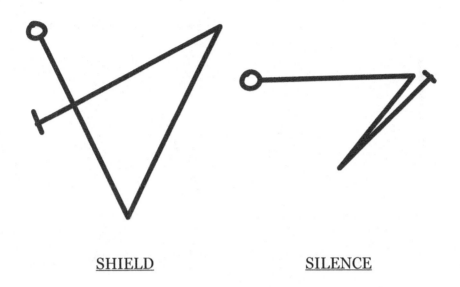

SHIELD                SILENCE

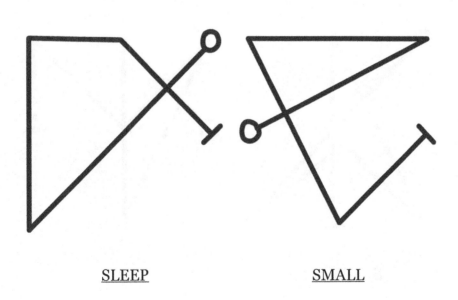

SLEEP                SMALL

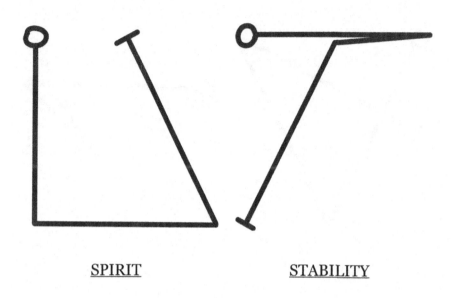

SPIRIT          STABILITY

STRENGTH          TIME

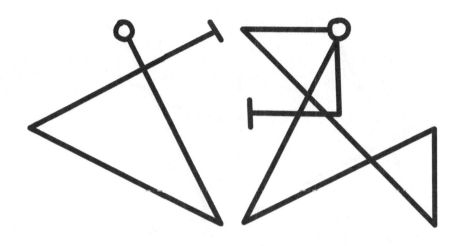

TRAVEL                    TREASURE

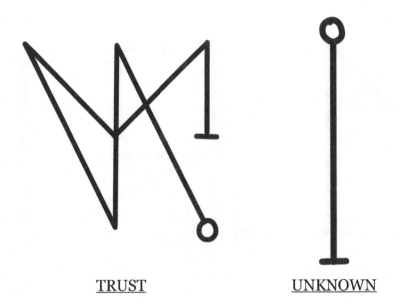

TRUST                    UNKNOWN

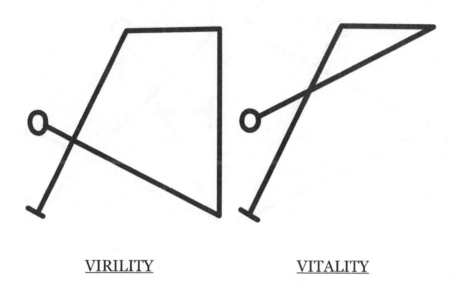

VIRILITY          VITALITY

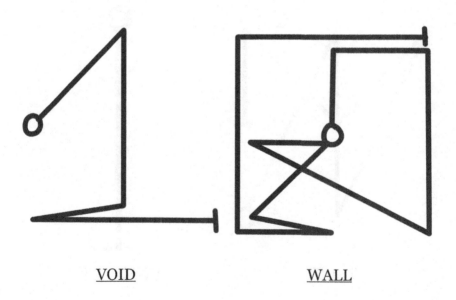

VOID          WALL

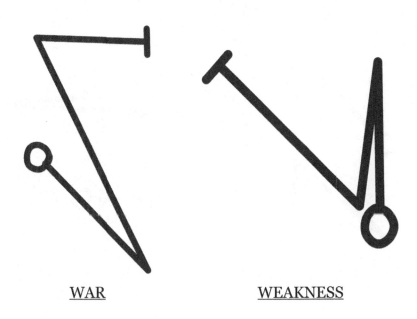

WAR                    WEAKNESS

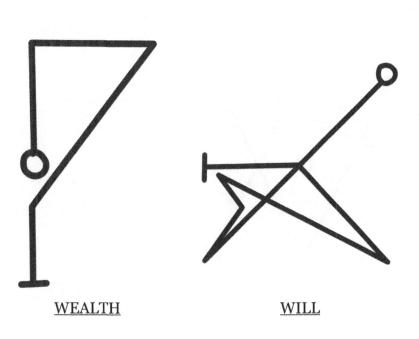

WEALTH                WILL

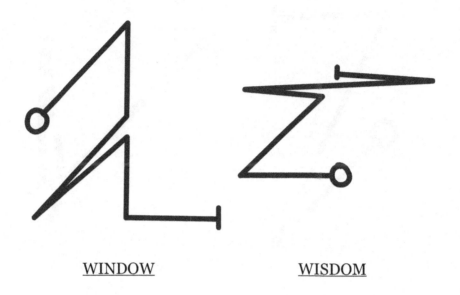

WINDOW          WISDOM

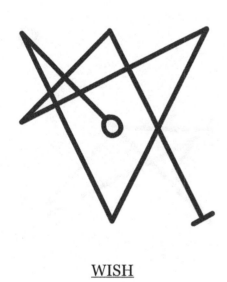

WISH

# PHYSICAL SIGILS

<u>Representations of Magick Tools</u>

ALTAR                    ATHAME

CANDLE                   CAULDRON

CHALICE                    CLOAK

CRYSTAL BALL               GRIMOIRE

143

INCENSE          PENDULUM

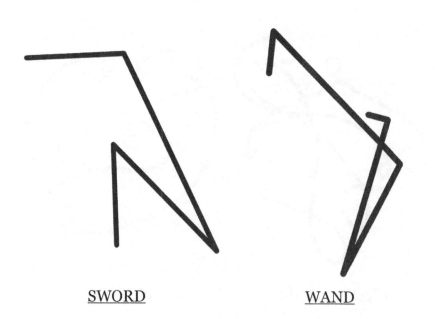

SWORD          WAND

# PHYSICAL SIGILS

For Divination

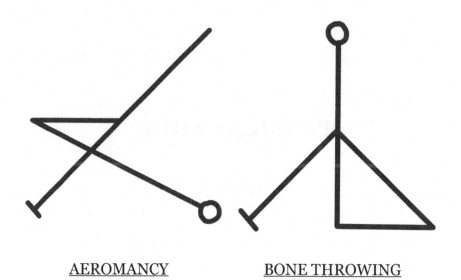

AEROMANCY                    BONE THROWING

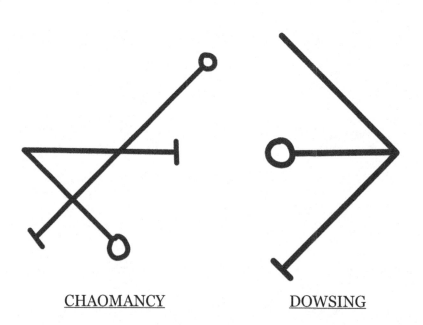

CHAOMANCY                    DOWSING

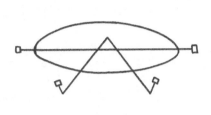

GENERAL
DIVINATION

GEOMANCY

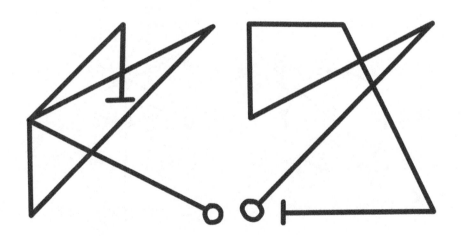

NECROMANCY

PALMISTRY

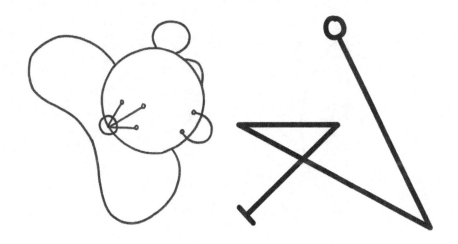

PROPHETIC DREAMS          RIBBON READING

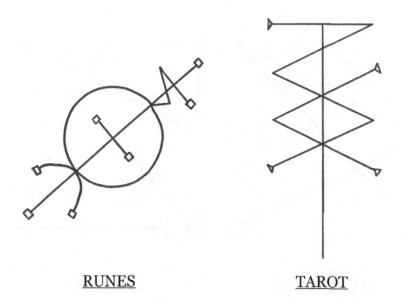

RUNES                    TAROT

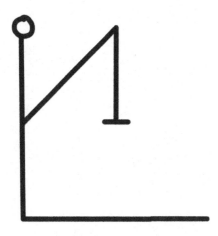

TASSEOGRAPHY

# PHYSICAL SIGILS

## For Protection

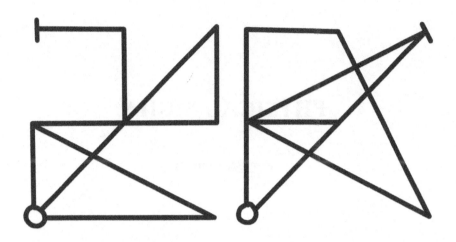

## FROM AGGRESSIVE ENTITIES

## DURING ASTRAL TRAVEL

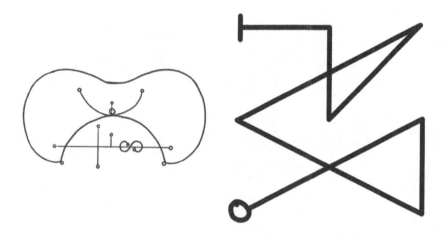

## FROM BAD DREAMS

## FROM DEMONIC ENTITIES

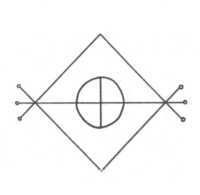

**GENERAL
PROTECTION**

**TO PROTECT
A HOME**

**FROM JINXES**

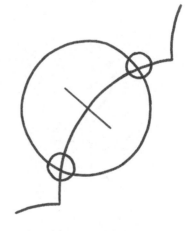

**FROM MALEVOLENT
SPIRITS**

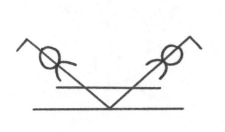

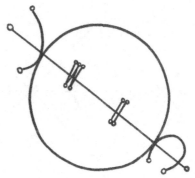

### FROM OFFENSIVE
### MAGICK

### TO PROTECT
### A PERSON

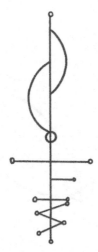

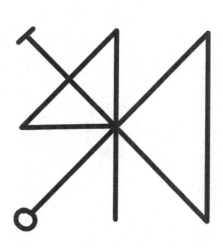

### TO PROTECT A ROOM,
### SPACE, OR AREA

### FROM WHAT ONE
### SUMMONS

# PHYSICAL SIGILS

## Representations of Creatures

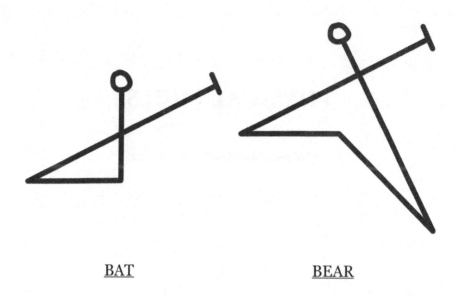

BAT

BEAR

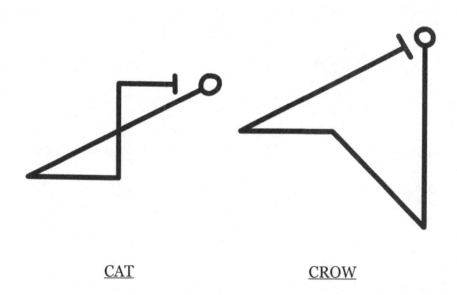

CAT

CROW

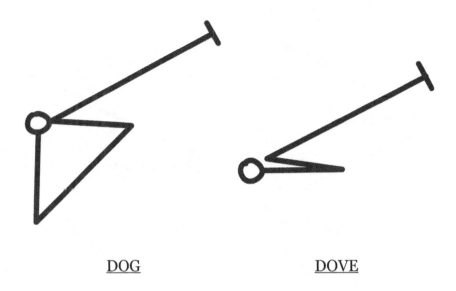

DOG DOVE

DRAGON FISH

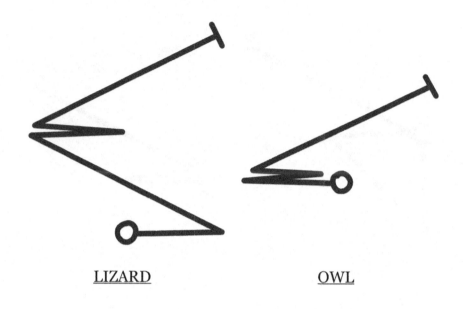

LIZARD                    OWL

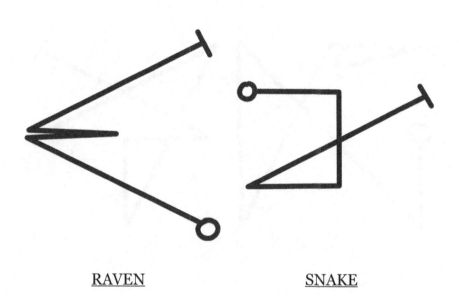

RAVEN                    SNAKE

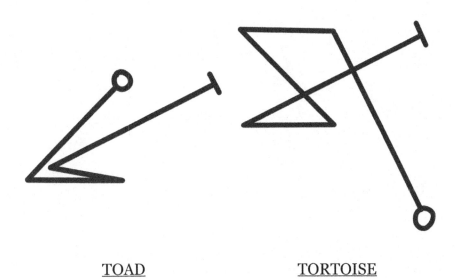

TOAD          TORTOISE

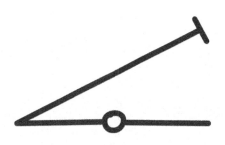

WOLF

# PHYSICAL SIGILS

## Representations of The Sabbaths

BELTANE                    IMBOLC

LAMMAS                    LITHA

MABON                OSTARA

SAMHAIN                YULE

# PHYSICAL SIGILS

## Representations of The Seven Deadly Sins

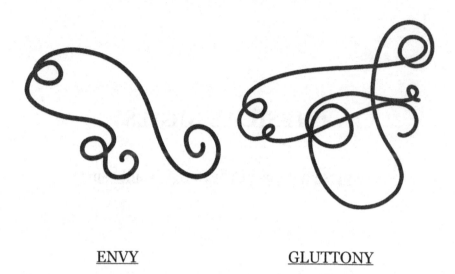

ENVY                    GLUTTONY

GREED                    LUST

PRIDE                    SLOTH

WRATH

# PHYSICAL SIGILS

## For Spells & Rituals

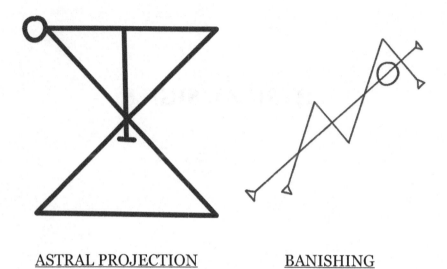

ASTRAL PROJECTION          BANISHING

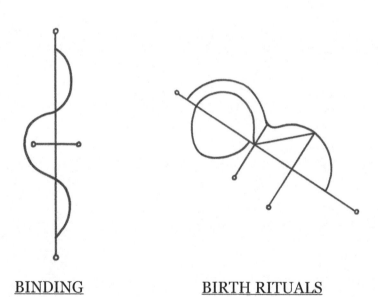

BINDING          BIRTH RITUALS

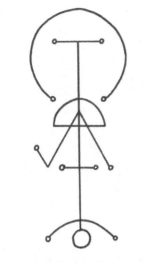

**CANDLE CHARGING**

**CANDLE MAGICK**

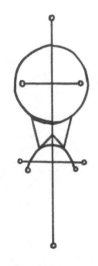

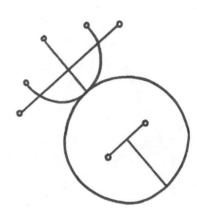

**CHARMWORK**

**CLEANSING**

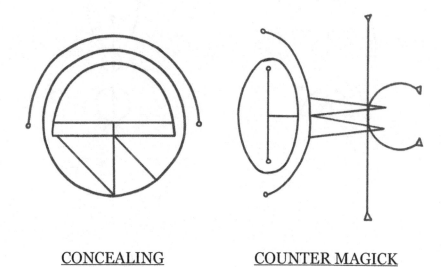

CONCEALING          COUNTER MAGICK

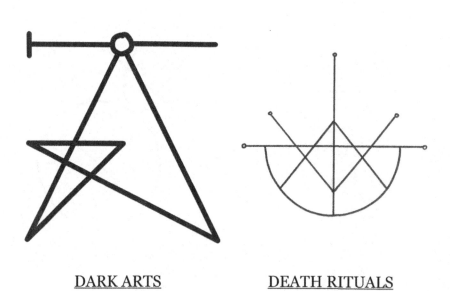

DARK ARTS          DEATH RITUALS

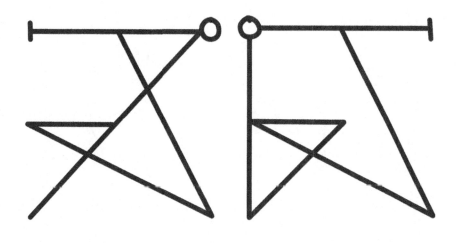

DESTRUCTION      DIMENSIONAL
                 JUMPING

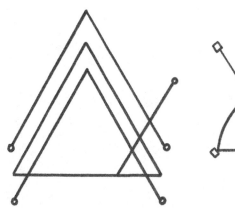

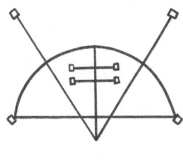

ELEMENTAL MAGICK      ELEMENTAL MAGICK
AIR                   EARTH

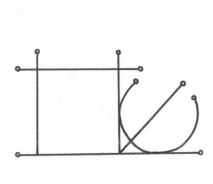

**ELEMENTAL MAGICK**
**FIRE**

**ELEMENTAL MAGICK**
**SPIRIT**

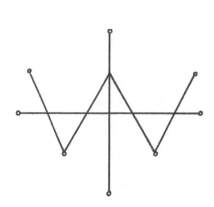

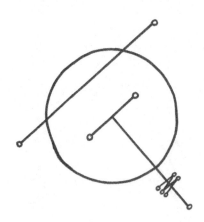

**ELEMENTAL MAGICK**
**WATER**

**EMOTIONS SPELLS**

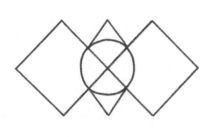

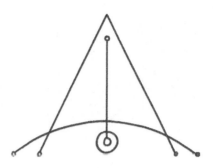

EMPOWERMENT

EVOCATION

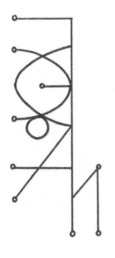

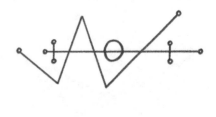

GLAMOUR

HEALING

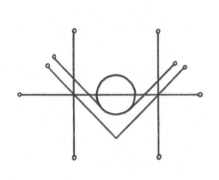

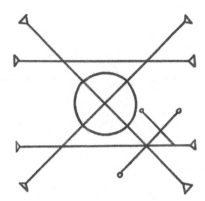

### HERBAL CHARGING

### HEX BREAKING

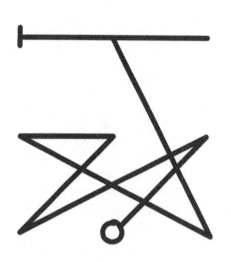

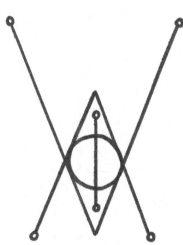

### HEXING

### INVOCATION

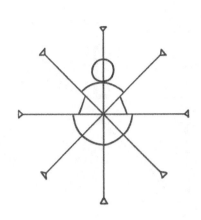

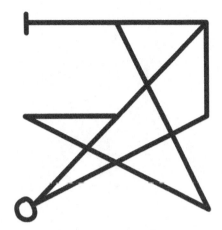

JINXES

LIFE RITUALS

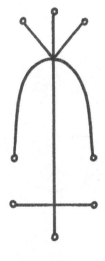

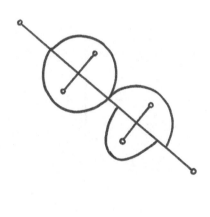

LUCK

LUST

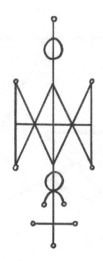

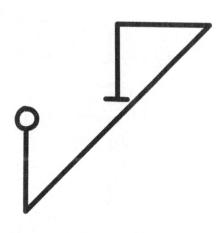

MANIFESTATION　　　MANIPULATION

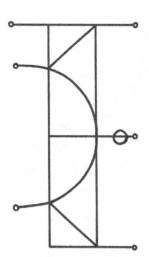

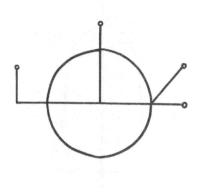

MARRIAGE RITUALS　　　OFFERING

POTENCY

PROSPERITY

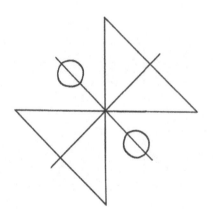

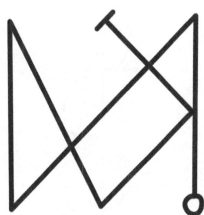

PROTECTION

REALITY SHIFT

179

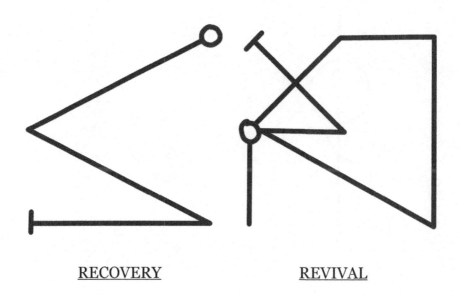

RECOVERY         REVIVAL

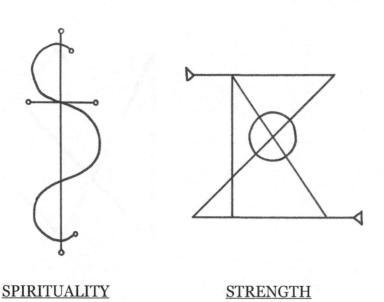

SPIRITUALITY         STRENGTH

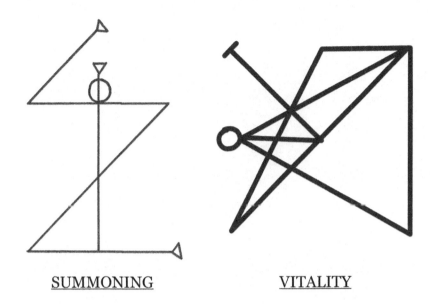

SUMMONING               VITALITY

Made in the USA
Las Vegas, NV
28 December 2023

83663780R00121